The Election Book

THE PEOPLE
★ ★ ★ PICK a ★ ★ ★
PRESIDENT

SCHOLASTIC
REFERENCE

* * * * * * * * * *

For the future voters and future presidents of the United States of America

Acknowledgments

Special thanks to Lee Kravitz for his support and encouragement when I was writing this book, to Carol Drisko and Steven Manning for sharing their expertise, and to the people at the *Congressional Quarterly* and the Federal Election Commission for their patient and prompt answers to all my questions.

....

Text by Tamara Henneman
Updated text for 2004 edition by Carolyn Jackson
Book design by Kay Petronio

0-439-68708-X

10 9 8 7 6 5 4 3 2 1   04 05 06 07 08

Printed in the U.S.A.

Updated edition, September 2004

CONTENTS

★ ★ ★ ★ ★ ★ ★ ★ ★ ★ ★

Preface

Every four years, Americans elect a new president. The election is the top story on television news shows and in newspapers nearly every day for a year leading up to the election. Yet most people don't know very much about how the election really works.

Since we have a government of the people, by the people, and for the people, it's important that people—including people like you—know what goes on in an election year. *The Election Book* tells the story. When you read it, you'll know more about choosing a president than most Americans. And although it may be a few years before you can vote, you'll be able to follow the news and understand what is happening today.

1
Government by the Voters

The United States is a democracy. This means that ordinary people decide who runs the government. Every four years Americans get to choose a president, the country's single-most powerful and important leader.

During an election year, all eyes are on the presidential candidates. The candidates are in the headlines and on the evening news. Everywhere you turn, you see a candidate's face on a poster, or name on a bumper sticker.

But the real power during the election is with the people. Each candidate, whether giving a speech, touring a factory, or appearing on television, has just one goal in an election year. That is to get the votes of the people.

The U.S. presidential election is probably the longest and the toughest race in the world to win. And the winner ends up with one of the toughest but most important jobs in the world. This book describes how a few Americans get into the race for president, and how millions of Americans take part in choosing the winner.

The Nation's Top Leader

2

W hen the people choose a president, they are choosing the person who will have the most powerful, prestigious, and difficult job in the country, maybe even in the world. From the Oval Office in the White House, the president carries out awesome responsibilities.

The President's Many Jobs

The president is the chief executive and heads the executive branch of the U.S. government. The president suggests laws to Congress that shape nearly every aspect of our society, from business to education, from housing to health care. He or she is "boss" to the millions of government workers who see that laws are carried out.

As chief of state, the president is the ultimate leader of the American people. He or she must inspire and lead the country through both good times and bad times.

The president is America's top diplomat, meeting with foreign leaders and deciding what the country's foreign policy will be.

Also commander-in-chief, the president is in charge of all U.S. armed forces—the Army, Navy, Air Force, and Marines.

The President's Top Advisors

To do each of these jobs, the president needs help from many experts in different fields, including international politics, education, economics, agriculture, transportation, and more. The president chooses 15 experts to be in the "Cabinet," his or her top group of advisors. These are people who have the president's deepest trust and highest respect.

When choosing a candidate for president, voters often consider who might be appointed to the Cabinet. They want to choose someone who is capable of doing all of the president's jobs well, and someone who will get the best advice.

George Washington's first cabinet meeting included secretaries of state, war (today called defense), and treasury. Later, he added the secretary of the navy and the attorney general, who was and is the nation's chief prosecutor. As the nation grew and government became more complicated, the cabinet was enlarged. By 2001, the cabinet of George W. Bush had fifteen members. Among them were Tom

Ridge, Secretary of the new Department of Homeland Security, and Colin Powell, the first African-American Secretary of State. Women have served in the cabinet since 1933, when President Franklin Roosevelt named Frances Perkins as Secretary of Labor. But all the members were white until 1966, when President Lyndon Johnson named African-American Robert Weaver to serve as Secretary of Housing and Urban Development.

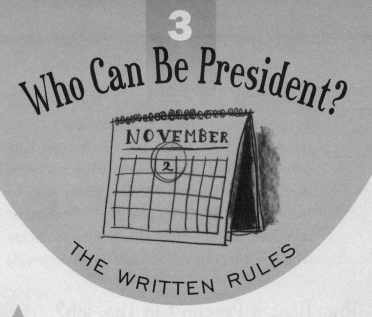

Who Can Be President?

THE WRITTEN RULES

If you look at the forty-three people who have had the job of president so far, you might think that only white males are allowed in the Oval Office. That's not true. There are very few rules about who can be president.

Who Is Eligible for the Job?

The Constitution, which is the set of rules defining our government, states only that the president must:

- be at least 35 years old.
- have lived in the United States for 14 years.
- be a "natural-born citizen" of the United States. (Basically, that means you have to be born in

the United States. Some people say you're also a "natural-born citizen" if at least one of your parents is a U.S. citizen, but your mother happened to be out of the country when you were born. No one born under these circumstances has ever tried to run for president. When someone does, the government will have to decide whether that person is a "natural-born citizen.")

How Does a Person Get the Job?

The Constitution also describes some surprising things about how a person can get the job of president. The most important day in an election year is the first Tuesday after the first Monday in November. That is Election Day, the day Americans vote for president. But what most people don't know, or what they forget, is that their votes do not directly elect the president. The Constitution says the Electoral College must choose the president.

Who Really Elects the President?

When the Constitution was written, the founders

worried that would-be tyrants would appeal to uneducated voters. To guard against this, they decided that the people would not directly elect the president and senators. In 1913, the Constitution was amended so that voters, not state legislatures, elected senators. However, the Constitution was left unchanged about the election of the president. It still says that a group of electors from each state, not the voters, select the president. Originally, these electors were educated men who were expected to use their independent judgment. Today, electors are expected to cast their ballots for the candidate who receives the most votes in their state on Election Day. Usually, that's what they do, but they are not legally bound in every state. Together, the electors are called the Electoral College. It is not a school, but a virtual group that meets in mid-December after a presidential election to cast its votes.

How the Electoral College Works

If you look at the ballot in a presidential election, you will see that electors are listed for each candidate. Technically, the voter selects the electors, not the presidential or vice presidential candidate. Many people have urged that the Constitution be amended so that the people directly elect the president. This is because it is possible for a candidate to receive the most popular votes and still lose in the Electoral College. This has happened four times in the nation's history. The last time was in 2000.

4

Who Can Be President?

THE UNWRITTEN RULES

O bviously, most of the qualities and qualifications that a candidate for president needs are not written in the laws of the land. Neither are many of the steps Americans take in choosing their top leader. There are many "unwritten" rules about who can become president and how they get the job. The American people decide what those rules are and change them slightly each time they elect a president.

In the 200 years since the Constitution was written, the standards by which Americans judge their presidential candidates have evolved and changed. So have the methods used to choose a person for the job. The serious contenders for the presidency know what the people expect from a leader, and they set out to prove they can do the job.

Experience

Candidates need the right kind of experience before people will consider them seriously as a potential president. People from many different professions go on to become presidents, but every president has had experience in government or experience leading a large organization before getting the country's top job.

Since the 1960s, many candidates for president have been governors and/or U.S. senators. Twenty-five presidents have been lawyers. Several—among them Washington, Jackson, Grant, and Eisenhower—have been military leaders. Others have been farmers, teachers, and businessmen. A former actor, Ronald Reagan, became one of our most popular presidents.

Courage and Conviction

A candidate for president must be convinced, beyond a doubt, that he or she is the best person for the job. To be president, a person needs powerful ideas about what he or she can do for the country and has to convince people to support these ideas.

During the campaign season, the whole country will judge both the candidates and their ideas. The country watches everything the candidates do. Journalists report on and question every decision candidates make during the campaign, and nearly every decision in their lives previous to the campaign. A candidate has to have courage to face the people's judgment during the campaign and the courage to lead them if he or she is elected.

Energy and Spirit

The campaign for president is long and grueling. Candidates travel all over the United States during the campaign, sometimes visiting five or more states a day. Most candidates for president are spouses and parents, too. They have to be away from their families and friends for weeks at a time. Even if candidates are exhausted and miss their families, they must keep their spirits up and show their best side.

Some people say the American election process is too long and too exhausting for the candidates. Others say that it is a good test to see if a person can withstand the rigors of being president.

Money

Campaigning for president takes lots of money. In 2000, the candidates spent a combined total of more than $607 million, and total federal campaign spending reached nearly $4 billion!

Party Favorites

Since 1852, no candidate has won a presidential election without first getting nominated for the job by either the Democratic Party or the Republican Party. These parties are the two major political organizations in the United States.

Political leaders began forming the parties more

than 100 years ago as a way of getting many people to support one person for president. Today, the two parties dominate our system of government. Each party has its own system for nominating and supporting a candidate for president. There are other, smaller, political parties, too. During many election years, new parties form to back a presidential candidate. One of the alternate or "third" parties can affect the election by drawing support away from the main parties, but the Democrats and the Republicans have the most power when it comes to electing a president.

Although the Constitution does not mention political parties, we have had national parties since 1800. Today, two parties—the Republicans and the Democrats—dominate our system of government. Each party has its own system for nominating and supporting its candidates. One of the unofficial roles of a president has been to head the party that elected him.

There are other, smaller political parties, too. These parties often form over issues that are "hot buttons." Among the ideas that have made their way into politics via small parties are the eight-hour workday, the direct election of senators, and the practice of recall and referendum in state elections. Former presidents Martin Van Buren, Millard Fillmore, and Theodore Roosevelt tried to make their way back into the White House through third parties, but they failed. In 2000, there were three candidates from minor parties—Pat Buchanan of the Reform Party, Harry Browne of the Libertarian Party, and Ralph Nader from the Green Party.

5
Party Power

Political parties are an important link between the voters and the candidates. They get many people involved in choosing candidates for president. They also organize people to support candidates, and help clarify the choice people have to make on Election Day.

Most candidates for president begin their political careers by working for one of the two main parties. They often campaign for other candidates before running for office themselves.

Democrat or Republican?

Each party has a platform, or a set of goals it works

for. Voters identify themselves as Democrats or Republicans depending on which party's goals they support. Even when voters do not consider themselves a member of either political party, they often vote for one of the party's candidates.

Today, almost all elected officials—from school board members to city council members to state legislators to governors to members of Congress— are members of political parties, usually Democrats or Republicans. On all levels, elected officials of the two major parties work together to achieve their party's goals.

The Democratic Party has been around since 1828. During the 1960s, the Democrats became known as the "liberal party" for their support of civil rights, organized labor, and Medicare. More recently, they have been more successful with centrist candidates, such as Jimmy Carter and Bill Clinton.

The Republican Party has been around since 1854, and calls itself the Grand Old Party, or GOP. As the party of Lincoln, Republicans favored the Union in the Civil War, and, later, Reconstruction of the South. However, since President Richard Nixon, the party has gained popularity among white voters in the South. Under President George W. Bush, it appealed to religious conservatives and those who opposed laws to compensate women and members of racial and ethnic minorities for past discrimination.

In practice, neither party can elect a president without the support of "swing voters" who look more to individual candidates than parties, and of independents with no declared party allegiance. Both parties must appeal to voters of racial minorities, to women, and to corporations that control much of the nation's economy.

Party Mascots

Both parties also have mascots, and you will see a lot of them during an election year. The Democrats have the donkey, and the Republicans have the elephant. Strangely enough, both symbols were first used to make fun of the parties, but party leaders managed to turn this to their own advantage.

Andrew Jackson started the Democratic Party in 1828 when he was running for president. Jackson's political foes said he was as stubborn and foolish as a mule. Jackson shrugged off the name-calling and began using drawings of donkeys on his campaign posters. He went on to win the election! Today, you still find the donkey on Democratic campaign posters, buttons, and bumper stickers.

A political cartoonist in the 1870s began using the elephant to stand for the Republicans, probably because the party was then the largest in the country. The reference was not a compliment, however. The cartoon showed the elephant getting scared off by a donkey in a lion costume! Nevertheless, some people in the party must have liked the image. The elephant became a symbol of the party and now marches across the posters, buttons, and other campaign paraphernalia of the Republicans.

The Pick of the Parties

A candidate's first goal is to win the nomination for president from one of the major political parties. To do this, he or she has to win the support of party leaders and voters in every state, one state at a time.

Early in an election year, the major political parties in each state hold either an election called a "primary" or a meeting called a "caucus." The primaries and caucuses let party leaders know who the people support for president. They also determine who will be sent to the party's national convention in the summer. These representatives are called delegates. At the convention, they will vote to choose the party's official nominee for president.

Primaries

A primary is a statewide election open to all members of the major political parties. Some states also have "open primaries" that people can vote in even if they are not a member of either political party. In most states, Republicans and Democrats have their primary elections on the same day. There can be many candidates running for each party's nomination. A voter must pick one candidate from *either* the Republican Party or the Democratic Party. They cannot vote in both primaries.

Although voters usually name a presidential candidate, what they are really doing is choosing delegates to go to the convention. Based on the primary vote totals, party leaders select delegates for the convention. The delegates are expected to represent the wishes expressed by the people's vote in the primary. In some states, people actually vote for the delegates instead of the presidential candidates.

Caucuses

Caucus meetings are like mini-elections in which only active party members can vote. Every state is divided into voting districts and precincts. Caucuses are meetings of all the active party members in a district or precinct. The party members vote for delegates to represent them at the convention, either knowing which candidate a delegate is likely to support or simply trusting in that delegate's judgment.

The state-by-state schedule for primaries and caucuses usually begins in February of an election year. Each week until June, a few states have their primaries or caucuses. During these five months, candidates rush from state to state, campaigning to win both the people's support and the support of the delegates who will attend the national conventions.

6

Deciding to Run

Potential candidates think long and hard before deciding to run for president. They must consider everything described to you so far. Can they expect support from people in their political party *and* from the American voters? Can they raise enough money? Do they have faith and confidence in themselves and in their views on this country? Are they and their families ready to enter the longest, hardest election race in the world?

Years before the election, potential candidates may begin to "test the waters" to see if they have a chance at becoming president. They talk with other powerful people in their political party. They let it be known that they are interested in running for president and try to build support from within the party.

Potential candidates also travel around the country, meeting people, giving speeches, and raising money for a campaign. It is important to see how people react to their ideas. They also want people to begin thinking about them as presidential material.

As the election year draws near, candidates begin to declare officially that they are running for president. Usually a candidate calls a press conference. In front of television cameras and news reporters, the candidate tells Americans, "I want to

be your next president." If the current president wants to be reelected, a press conference is held to announce the decision.

From this point on, candidates are no longer "testing the waters." They are in the race.

The Campaign Team

Candidates for president put together a team of people to help them run for office. A candidate hires a campaign manager to oversee every part of the campaign. Schedulers decide where and when candidates will meet the voters. "Advance people" make sure a candidate's supporters are on hand at each scheduled campaign stop. Press secretaries make sure the news reporters show up. Pollsters survey Americans to see how the candidate is doing. In an election year, dozens of people have full-time jobs helping the candidates.

A president seeking reelection puts together a campaign team, too. A president has many advantages over other candidates in the race. The president is already familiar to Americans.

Whenever the president does something even just a little bit interesting, it's on the news. But running for office from the White House is also very demanding. Often there are arguments and tensions between the campaign team and the regular advisors. They both want all of the president's time.

7

The Long Campaign

Usually, campaigning begins months—or even years—before the first primary. Candidates raise money, meet with potential supporters, and appear on television whenever possible. In 2004, the Internet became a tool for political parties and candidates as never before.

The Cash

Almost from the second a person begins thinking about the presidency, money is an issue. Where will it come from? Individual donors, special-interest groups, corporations, and even the government itself are possible sources. Each, however, comes with its own limitations.

Candidates are eager to raise money, and many people are eager to influence them. Campaign reformers try to measure the influence of money by tracking where it comes from and how it is spent. They believe that unidentified donations are a threat to democracy, because voters cannot judge the interests of the donors. In 1971, after the Watergate scandal, Congress passed the first Federal Election Campaign Act to keep track of federal contributions. Although the act was amended twice, candidates and contributors found ways to pump ever-increasing and unidentified dollars into campaigns.

In 2002, Congress passed the Bipartisan Campaign Reform Act. It banned "soft" money—contributions to political parties from corporations, labor unions, and wealthy individuals that parties could use any way they wanted. Soft money had been used by groups to pay for anonymous ads on particular issues just before an election. The reform act said that each person could donate $2,000 in "hard" money directly to a presidential or senate candidate in each election (primary and general) and $1,000 to a candidate running for U.S. representative. It also said that people too young to vote could not contribute. These laws were challenged by groups as opposite as the Chamber of Commerce and the unions of the AFL-CIO. But the courts upheld the "soft" money rule, and extended the ban on anonymous "issue ads" beyond the time around elections. One part they did overturn was the restriction on "hard" money contributions by minors. Today, even if you can't vote, you can give up to $2,000 to your favorite candidate for president or senator and up to $1,000 to a prospective U.S. representative.

In the 2000 election, only twelve percent of eligible voters contributed any money. But at least fifty donors gave $1 million or more in "soft" money. In 2004, that loophole will be closed. Candidates will have to decide if they can raise the money they need by themselves, or if they want to take government funds collected when taxpayers check off a dollar donation on their income tax returns. If candidates take federal funds, they will have to agree to a limit on spending.

Running a campaign is incredibly expensive. Candidates have to pay salaries to their staffs and must also pay the expense of traveling with their staffs. Advertising is the biggest campaign expense. Ads in newspapers and billboards and on radio and television cost tens of millions of dollars.

In 1999, George W. Bush raised $37 million before June 30. That was equal to the total raised by the ten other Republican candidates, or by Democrats Bill Bradley and Al Gore combined. This early start in fund-raising helps explain how Bush won the Republican nomination, and then the presidency.

Meeting People

Candidates travel from state to state, giving speeches and meeting people. They try to tell as many people as they can about how they would make the country better if they were elected president. During the primaries, Democrats are running against Democrats and Republicans against Republicans. So each candidate tries to convince voters that he or she is the party's best hope for beating the other party.

Candidates go to schools, shopping malls, factories, farms, and town hangouts like bowling alleys and cafés. Shaking hands and kissing babies are two time-honored methods candidates use to show that they really care about people. It may sound silly, but wouldn't you like to shake the hand of the next president?

The Internet

In the 1980s, personal computers became familiar household objects. But not until the 1990s did the technology to use those computers to communicate become available. First, there was electronic mail, or e-mail. Then people everywhere were able to log on to the World Wide Web. There they could get news and information instantly from around the world. It took politicians a while to use this new technology.

The Web created a new medium for communicating with many people without the permission of any large organization. Anyone could register a site, and many people did. During the campaign to impeach President Bill Clinton in 1998–99, Web journalist Matt Drudge and others regularly posted news and rumors on a popular Web site, but there was little response from the White House.

Under George W. Bush, however, the White House has developed direct communication, including on-line chats, with citizens via the Internet. And in 2002, Democratic primary candidate Howard Dean used the Internet to mobilize early support and secure on-line donations. That support, however, did not translate into enough votes to win the nomination. Some observers said that the introduction of the Internet into politics would be as revolutionary as television when it was first used in the early 1960s. Like television, the Internet allows candidates to reach out to voters that they cannot meet in person. And, it's a lot cheaper.

Television

No matter how much they travel, candidates can't meet everyone. So, they spend a lot of time trying to get television cameras and news photographers to cover their activities. This leads them to do some pretty silly stunts. Candidates are always marching through factories wearing hard hats or traipsing through farmyards petting the livestock, hoping the press will record them in these unusual settings. And they spend millions on television commercials and newspaper ads in order to promote their image and get their message across to voters.

Debates

A candidate may also agree to debate with other candidates. Debates are one sure-fire way to get on television. They give candidates the chance to let people know their views on important topics. Candidates also have a chance to meet and respond to each other in front of millions of voters.

Opinion Polls

A candidate's pollsters survey Americans to figure out what issues are important to people and what topics the candidate should talk about in speeches. The polls are also a way for the candidate to make the news. If a survey shows the candidate far ahead of his or her opponents in the eyes of American voters, the candidate's press secretary might release the results to reporters and hope it makes headlines. Newspapers and television stations also take their own surveys to find out which candidate the American people like best.

The Field Narrows

If a party has a first-term president in the White House, it rarely has to worry about finding another candidate. Time, energy, and money spent gathering a nomination can be saved. But if a president is serving a second term, the party must look for a new candidate. You can be sure the "out" party is busy doing the same thing. In early February 2004, there were six Democratic candidates actively campaigning to face Republican George W. Bush in November, and four more had already dropped out.

After the first month of primaries, the field usually begins to narrow. People who don't win at least a few early primaries and caucuses usually drop out of the race. New Hampshire holds the first primary election in the country, and Iowa holds the first caucus. News reporters pay a lot of attention to candidates who win these early races. This media attention can strengthen their campaigns.

In early March there is an important primary day called Super Tuesday. Many states in the South and a few others have primaries or caucuses on this day. A candidate who doesn't do well on Super Tuesday may drop out, too.

8
Party Conventions

The Republican and Democratic parties each have a rowdy summertime meeting called a "convention." This is where their final choice for president is made. By the time of the convention, there are usually only two or three candidates left in the race for each party's nomination. Often, one of those candidates is the clear front-runner for the nomination and has the support of plenty of delegates.

At convention time, all the delegates chosen in primaries and caucuses, and the powerful leaders from each party, gather. They meet in a large space in a big city so that there are plenty of hotel rooms and restaurants. In 2004, the Democrats held their convention on July 26–29 in Boston's FleetCenter. That's where the Celtics play basketball and the Bruins play hockey. Republicans gathered from August 20–September 2, in New York's Madison Square Garden. The New York Knicks play basketball in the Garden, and many large rock concerts are held there, too.

Party members do three important jobs at the conventions: decide on a party platform, nominate a president, and nominate a vice president. It sounds like very official business, and it is. But it is conducted in a circus-like atmosphere.

Conventions are a time for political party members to blow off steam after the primary campaigns, to meet and celebrate, and to show the whole country how spirited, enthusiastic, and confident they are. In short, each party uses this opportunity to make an incredible spectacle of itself.

Conventions last about three days. They open with a round of rousing speeches. Officials from the host city and state give welcoming speeches. Top party officials also speak. Then, a party leader gives the keynote address. This is an especially important speech. It dramatically sets forth the themes the party wants to stress and helps set the tone of the whole convention. As with all major events of the convention, planners try to schedule the keynote address during prime time for the television networks. That's usually around 8 P.M. eastern time. All the major networks broadcast the speech live.

The Platform

The first piece of major business is to adopt a platform. This is a statement of the party's goals and principles. A committee brings a draft of the platform to the convention, and "planks" or ideas are added or changed, until, finally, a majority of delegates vote to accept the platform.

Choosing the Candidate

Next, the convention moves on to the moment everyone has been waiting for: picking the nominee for president of the United States. Delegates from each state have been assigned banks of seats in the convention hall. Many dress in red, white, and blue, wear funny hats, and wave banners and posters for the candidate they support.

Candidates are officially nominated by prominent party members, to the resounding cheers of their supporters. Then, state by state, each bank of delegates is called upon. With a flourish, one delegate will stand and announce the vote of that state's delegates, stating how many delegate votes go to each candidate who is up for nomination. In the first round of voting, the delegates are expected to vote for the candidate they had pledged to support during the party's primaries and caucuses. However, each party also sends delegates to the convention who are officially "uncommitted." They can vote for whomever they wish.

If one candidate gets a majority—or more than half—of the votes, then that candidate is the party's choice. If no candidate gets at least half of the votes, nominations are taken again. A candidate's supporters double their efforts to gain support before a second round of state-by-state balloting. If a candidate still does not get a majority of votes, another round of nominating and balloting is held. This will go on until one candidate wins a majority of the delegate votes and becomes the party's nominee for president.

After the first round of balloting, delegates are no longer bound to vote for the candidate they were pledged to in their state's primary or caucus. They can vote for whomever they think is the best candidate. Party leaders may choose to nominate someone who did not even run in the primaries or caucuses. A convention in which party leaders "draft" a candidate who did not run in the primaries, and get that candidate nominated by the party, is called a "brokered" convention.

Choosing the Vice President

Before any balloting takes place, candidates for the presidency usually announce who they want to run with them for the office of vice president. After the delegates choose a presidential nominee, they vote for the vice president, but balloting this time around is really just a formality. Everyone assumes that the delegates will vote for the candidate the presidential nominee wants as a running mate.

Choosing a vice president is often an opportunity for a presidential candidate to bridge gaps and mend fences with people in the party who do not enthusiastically support him or her. In 1980, Ronald Reagan and George Bush both ran for the Republican nomination for president. They waged an intense fight against each other that had many in the party angry. By asking George Bush to be his running mate, the front-runner Ronald Reagan reunited his party.

Hoopla to the Last

In closing the convention, the candidates for the top two offices in the land give acceptance speeches. Again, convention planners make every effort to schedule the speeches during prime-time television viewing hours, so that as many Americans as possible will see the candidates. The delegates and other people at the convention keep cheering, waving banners, and throwing confetti until the end. They want to show the country how psyched they are to get their candidate into office!

The Big Show

W hen the political conventions are over, both major parties have their candidates. There may be a break in the campaigning until after Labor Day.

This is not necessarily a calm period for the candidates and their parties. There is a lot of work to be done. If the fight for the nomination has been a bitter one, the candidate tries to reunite his or her party for the big push ahead. There is poll-taking to find out what the voters are thinking. There are meetings with consultants and strategists to refine and polish the candidate's message and plan the campaign. What are the candidate's strengths? What are the opponent's weaknesses? What is the best way to show off both to the voters? What will the campaign slogans be?

Money

During the general election campaign, the government gives each candidate from the two major parties the same amount of money to spend. In 2000, both major party nominees got $67.56 million from the federal treasury. Once a candidate accepts federal funds, he or she must agree not to spend more than that. However, both George W. Bush and Democratic Vice President Al Gore had already spent the money they raised, so the federal funds paid for 35 percent of Bush's campaign and 62.5 percent of Gore's.

The Two-Person Race

After Labor Day, campaigning begins again. The candidates resume their hectic travel schedules, again trying to meet as many voters as possible. This time around, candidates spend most of their time in the big states, where most of the voters are, and in states where the contest might be a close one. The big states have the most votes in the Electoral College. The candidates are trying to rack up enough electoral votes to win.

Now that it's a one-on-one fight, a candidate may change his or her approach to the voters. For one thing, the candidate now needs to appeal to all Americans, not just to those within his or her political party. A candidate's speeches and public appearances are designed to appeal to the broadest possible spectrum of American voters.

Getting Out the Vote

The political parties kick into high gear behind their candidate. During election years, political party members are active in nearly every city, town, and neighborhood in the United States

Volunteers go door to door in their neighborhood, trying to convince people to support their candidate on Election Day. They call people on the phone to gather support. They pass out leaflets, bumper stickers, and buttons with their candidate's name on them.

Party activists try to "get out the vote." They know that many Americans who are eligible often don't vote. Fifty-one percent of eligible U.S. voters cast a ballot in 2000, and only forty-nine percent did in 1996.

Every U.S. citizen over the age of 18 can vote if he or she is registered. You are a citizen if you were born here. You can also become a citizen if you moved here from another country. Registering just means signing up to vote.

The political parties and other organizations, such as the League of Women Voters, try to convince all Americans to vote. They make it easy to register by setting up registration booths at stores, parks, and other public places. They give elderly or disabled people rides to voting places. They babysit for young children so that their parents can go to vote.

What Really Happens

on Election Day

At last, Election Day arrives. The campaigning is over. The frenzy of activity, the speeches, the promises, and the television commercials have all stopped. Traditionally, candidates do not campaign on Election Day. They do what millions of other Americans do. They vote and then watch reports of the election on television.

Americans Go to the Polls

Every neighborhood or precinct has its own voting place, or poll. Usually, voting booths are set up in a public school, a firehouse, or the town hall. It is very likely that voting takes place in your school!

First, each voter must check in and prove he or she is registered to vote in that neighborhood. In some states, voters can register to vote right at the polling place on Election Day.

Traditionally, the voter goes into a space enclosed by a curtain. Inside is a machine to record the person's vote. That vote remains secret unless the voter tells someone.

If voters are away from home on Election Day, they can still cast a ballot. They have to get a special form, called an "absentee ballot," and mail it to the election office in their county.

In most elections, including the presidential elections, voters also choose people to fill more than one office. U.S. representatives run every two years, U.S. senators run every six years, and there may be a host of state and local candidates, plus issues such as permission to issue bonds.

In the 2004 Democratic primaries, Wisconsin experimented with allowing people to cast their votes through personal computers before Election Day. But no such plans were announced for the general election.

Counting Up the Votes

Local election officials at every voting place make sure things run smoothly and according to law. The officials are usually volunteers from both the Democratic and Republican parties. They record the votes counted by each voting machine and report them to a central election office. Officials from both parties are at the polling places to make sure that all votes are recorded and reported properly.

Some polling places have machines that punch a hole in a cardboard ballot card each time someone votes. At the end of Election Day, the officials take the cards to the central election office. Officials feed the cards into a computer that totals up the holes—votes—for each candidate, the same way a computer tallies up the answers. In 2000, Florida voters used a ballot that required punching out a hole beside the name of the desired candidate. That election was extremely close, and when the ballots were examined to re-count them, it was discovered that the holes were confusing to voters, and many had not been punched all the way through. An incomplete punch was referred to as a "hanging chad."

Some kinds of voting machines tally votes mechanically. Voters push levers next to the name of the candidate they support. Inside the machine there is a counter for each candidate. It looks just like the mileage counter on a car's dashboard. When the election officials open the machine, they write down the number of votes for each candidate on an official form. They take the form to the central election office where votes from all polling places are tallied up.

The most modern kind of voting machine is like a computer. It counts votes electronically. The candidates' names appear on a screen and voters push a button under the name of the candidate they support. The machine sends the vote count over a wire to a data center that tallies votes from many machines.

At each central counting place, officials add up the votes from machines in their area. When officials at a state office add all the totals together, the winner of the election in that state is known!

Prime-Time Results

The major television channels begin reporting on the

election early in the evening of Election Day. If you were thinking about watching your favorite show on this night, forget about it! All the major networks have their cameras turned on the most exciting show in the country: the presidential election.

As soon as possible, news organizations start collecting vote tallies from central election offices. They also conduct "exit polls." They ask voters leaving the polls who they voted for, and feed the results into a computer. Everyone wants to be first with the news. In 2000, the polls closed in eleven states by 7 P.M., Eastern Standard Time (EST). George W. Bush seemed to have an early lead. But at 8 P.M. the Voter News Service—working for ABC, NBC, CBS, CNN, Fox, and the AP—declared Al Gore the winner in Florida, and the news was announced. At 8:30 P.M., it appeared that Gore might win the presidency quickly, but Bush told reporters that he thought the networks had called the election too early. At 10:13 P.M., the Voter News Service took back its call in Florida. By 11 P.M., it appeared that the election was too close to call. All night long, the lead switched between candidates. By morning, it was clear that the election had been one of the closest in history, although several newspaper headlines proclaimed "Bush Wins!" It was thirty-six days before that news was official.

Afterwards, CNN hired a panel to report on the reporters. It scolded the networks for putting too much confidence in experts and polls. It said the Voter News Service used outdated technology. It suggested that the networks' practice of using key precincts to predict winners was not reliable. As a result, CNN said it would no longer use exit polls to call close races. It promised to fund a new precinct-sampling system.

Prime-Time Arguments

This was not the first time that the networks were accused of announcing a winner too soon. In 1980, long before people had finished voting, television reporters predicted that Ronald Reagan would beat President Jimmy Carter. Exit polls in the East showed Reagan a clear winner long before polls had closed in the West, where there is a three-hour time lag. Carter conceded at 9:45 P.M., EST. The speech was aired in the West before the polls closed.

There were many candidates on the ballot besides those for president. These candidates in western states were mad. Once people knew that Reagan had won, many registered voters did not bother to go to the polls. Candidates charged that the early announcement unfairly affected the outcome of other races.

Surveys taken after the 1980 election showed that people all over the country were upset by early reporting. Congress held hearings on the issue. Some people suggested closing all the polls at the same time. Others said they should be open twenty-four hours on Election Day. Still others asked Congress to stop the networks from broadcasting early results. But news organizations claimed that the First Amendment right of a free press allows them to decide how to report information that they gather.

After the 2000 election, CNN agreed not to call winners when polls in some states are still open. Other networks may follow suit, but they are not legally bound to. Watch your favorite station in the upcoming election to see if the coverage improves.

The Loser and the Winner Speak

Unless the election is close, one of the candidates usually admits defeat by 11 P.M., if not sooner. In each candidate's home state, hundreds of supporters have gathered in hotels. At this time, with the cameras rolling, the losing candidate gives a speech congratulating the winner and thanking supporters for all of their hard work. There is usually a lot of crying and booing in the audience. Shortly after, the winner appears in front of his or her party and gives a rousing speech to a shrieking, cheering, jubilant crowd.

Now everyone knows who the next president will be, but there is one more hurdle to jump before the results are official. The votes of the people do not directly elect the president. The Electoral College does.

11

The Electoral College

The Electoral College votes in mid-December. Each state gets as many electors in the Electoral College as it has senators and representatives in Congress. The District of Columbia gets three, for a total of 538. (How electors are chosen is up to the individual states.)

The electors meet at their state capitals. They each write their choice for president on a paper ballot and put it in a locked box. The boxes go to the Capitol Building in Washington, D.C. On January 6, the president of the Senate opens and counts the electoral votes in front of all the members of the House of Representatives and the Senate. A candidate needs a majority, or 270, electoral votes to win.

Electors are expected to vote for the candidate who got the most votes from the people of their state. Some states have laws that require electors to vote that way. It's a "winner-take-all" system. For example, California is a very big state and has fifty-five electors in the Electoral College. The candidate who wins the most votes from the people of California will get all fifty-five of California's electoral votes—even if the people's vote count was very close.

In very rare cases, one or a few electors have voted for a candidate who did not win in their state. They are called the "faithless electors." These electors have cast their votes as a protest. They have never intended to or succeeded in changing the outcome of an election.

Usually, the Electoral College votes, and then the votes are counted without people taking much notice. Newspapers and television stations report the events in passing.

Ties and Three-Way Races

If no candidate gets a majority of the votes in the Electoral College, then the House of Representatives decides who the winner is. This can happen if there is a tie or if there are three candidates in the race and none of them gets more than half of the electoral vote. Each state can cast just one vote. To be elected president by the House, a candidate has to get 26 votes.

If no vice-presidential candidate gets a majority of votes in the Electoral College, then the Senate chooses between the two candidates with the most votes. In this case, each Senator gets one vote.

Only two presidential elections have been decided by the House of Representatives. Thomas Jefferson won in the House in 1800, and John Quincy Adams in 1824.

Electoral Controversies

It is possible for a candidate to win the most votes from the people in the November election, but lose the race in the Electoral College! This can happen if the candidate loses in big electoral states by a very small number of votes, but wins in small electoral states by a very large number of votes.

In the 1800s, three candidates lost in the general election, but won the presidency after the Electoral

College voted. In 1824, Andrew Jackson won the most votes in the general election, but the Electoral College chose John Quincy Adams for president. In 1876, Samuel Tilden won the general election, but some votes were contested and there were charges of fraud. A special commission was set up to choose the president. After months of debate, the commission chose Tilden's opponent, Rutherford B. Hayes. In 1888, Grover Cleveland got the most popular votes, but Benjamin Harrison won in the Electoral College and became president.

As you know, the 2000 presidential election was very close. It took five weeks and a decision by the U.S. Supreme Court to determine the outcome. In the end, a recount of Florida ballots was stopped, and the state with its twenty-five electoral votes went to George W. Bush. Although Al Gore won the popular vote by 50,996,582 to 50,456,062, Bush won in the Electoral College, 271 to 266.

Today, some people think that the Electoral College should be abolished. They think a direct election by the U.S. people would be more democratic. But changing the system would mean amending the Constitution, and such an amendment has never gotten enough support to become law.

12

The New President

and the Next President

Almost immediately after the election is over, the losing party starts planning for next time. The search is on for a likely candidate. Presidential "wannabes" start putting out the word that they are interested in the job.

On January 20, after Election Day, the winner of the presidential election stands before the Chief Justice of the United States and takes the Oath of Office. At that moment, the winner of the toughest race to run becomes president of the United States.

Selected Election Web Sites

⊚ **KidsandPolitics.org**

http://www.kidsandpolitics.org

Profiles of the candidates and how they rate on issues relating to kids.

....

⊚ **Kids Voting USA**

http://www.kidsvotingusa.org

Test your knowledge of the Constitution and share your wishes for our country with other kids.

....

⊚ **The PBS Kids Democracy Project**

http://www.pbs.org/democracy/kids

How does government affect me? What's it like to be president for a day? Register your vote about issues such as the environment and health care.

Scholastic.com

http://www.teacher.scholastic.com/activities/election2004

Keep up with the latest election news reported by kids from all over the nation. Cast your vote in the site's election.

Young Politicians of America

http://www.ypa.org

Start your own political career at Young Politicians of America, devoted to learning about government through community service.